Elisha D. Smith Public Library

Menasha, Wisconsin 54952

DEMCO

By Seamus Heaney

The Haw Lantern

The Haw Lantern
Seamus Heaney

Farrar Straus Giroux

New York

First published in 1987 by Faber and Faber Limited, London
First American printing, 1987
Printed in the United States of America
Library of Congress Cataloging-in-Publication Data
Heaney, Seamus.
The haw lantern.
I. Title.
PR6058.E2H34   1987   821'.914   87-17705

Acknowledgments are due to the editors of the following
magazines where some of these poems appeared for the first
time: *Field, Gown, Harper's, Harvard Magazine, Honest Ulsterman,
Ireland of the Welcomes, Irish Times, London Review of Books,
Numbers, Ploughshares, Poetry Book Society Supplement, Poetry
Ireland Review, The Scotsman, Seneca Review, Threepenny Review,
Times Literary Supplement, Verse*. Nine of the poems appeared
in *Hailstones* (Gallery Press, 1984). An earlier version of the
sequence 'Clearances' was published in a limited edition by
Cornamona Press in 1986. 'From the Republic of
Conscience' was published as a pamphlet by Amnesty
International, Irish Section, on Human Rights Day, 1985.
'Alphabets' was the Phi Beta Kappa poem at Harvard
University in 1984. 'Parable Island' was written for William
Golding and included in *William Golding, The Man and his
Books: A Tribute on his 75th Birthday* (Faber and Faber, 1986);
'The Disappearing Island' was first read at a dinner for Tim
Severin organized by the St Brendan Society.

For Bernard and Jane McCabe

The riverbed, dried-up, half-full of leaves.
Us, listening to a river in the trees.

Contents

The Haw Lantern

Alphabets

I

A shadow his father makes with joined hands
And thumbs and fingers nibbles on the wall
Like a rabbit's head. He understands
He will understand more when he goes to school.

There he draws smoke with chalk the whole first week,
Then draws the forked stick that they call a Y.
This is writing. A swan's neck and swan's back
Make the 2 he can see now as well as say.

Two rafters and a cross-tie on the slate
Are the letter some call *ah*, some call *ay*.
There are charts, there are headlines, there is a right
Way to hold the pen and a wrong way.

First it is 'copying out', and then 'English'
Marked correct with a little leaning hoe.
Smells of inkwells rise in the classroom hush.
A globe in the window tilts like a coloured O.

II

Declensions sang on air like a *hosanna*
As, column after stratified column,
Book One of *Elementa Latina*,
Marbled and minatory, rose up in him.

For he was fostered next in a stricter school
Named for the patron saint of the oak wood
Where classes switched to the pealing of a bell
And he left the Latin forum for the shade

Of new calligraphy that felt like home.
The letters of this alphabet were trees.
The capitals were orchards in full bloom,
The lines of script like briars coiled in ditches.

Here in her snooded garment and bare feet,
All ringleted in assonance and woodnotes,
The poet's dream stole over him like sunlight
And passed into the tenebrous thickets.

He learns this other writing. He is the scribe
Who drove a team of quills on his white field.
Round his cell door the blackbirds dart and dab.
Then self-denial, fasting, the pure cold.

By rules that hardened the farther they reached north
He bends to his desk and begins again.
Christ's sickle has been in the undergrowth.
The script grows bare and Merovingian.

III

The globe has spun. He stands in a wooden O.
He alludes to Shakespeare. He alludes to Graves.
Time has bulldozed the school and school window.
Balers drop bales like printouts where stooked sheaves

Made lambdas on the stubble once at harvest
And the delta face of each potato pit
Was patted straight and moulded against frost.
All gone, with the omega that kept

Watch above each door, the good luck horse-shoe.
Yet shape-note language, absolute on air
As Constantine's sky-lettered IN HOC SIGNO
Can still command him; or the necromancer

Who would hang from the domed ceiling of his house
A figure of the world with colours in it
So that the figure of the universe
And 'not just single things' would meet his sight

When he walked abroad. As from his small window
The astronaut sees all he has sprung from,
The risen, aqueous, singular, lucent O
Like a magnified and buoyant ovum –

Or like my own wide pre-reflective stare
All agog at the plasterer on his ladder
Skimming our gable and writing our name there
With his trowel point, letter by strange letter.

Terminus

I

When I hoked there, I would find
An acorn and a rusted bolt.

If I lifted my eyes, a factory chimney
And a dormant mountain.

If I listened, an engine shunting
And a trotting horse.

Is it any wonder when I thought
I would have second thoughts?

II

When they spoke of the prudent squirrel's hoard
It shone like gifts at a nativity.

When they spoke of the mammon of iniquity
The coins in my pockets reddened like stove-lids.

I was the march drain and the march drain's banks
Suffering the limit of each claim.

III

Two buckets were easier carried than one.
I grew up in between.

My left hand placed the standard iron weight.
My right tilted a last grain in the balance.

Baronies, parishes met where I was born.
When I stood on the central stepping stone

I was the last earl on horseback in midstream
Still parleying, in earshot of his peers.

From the Frontier of Writing

The tightness and the nilness round that space
when the car stops in the road, the troops inspect
its make and number and, as one bends his face

towards your window, you catch sight of more
on a hill beyond, eyeing with intent
down cradled guns that hold you under cover

and everything is pure interrogation
until a rifle motions and you move
with guarded unconcerned acceleration –

a little emptier, a little spent
as always by that quiver in the self,
subjugated, yes, and obedient.

So you drive on to the frontier of writing
where it happens again. The guns on tripods;
the sergeant with his on-off mike repeating

data about you, waiting for the squawk
of clearance; the marksman training down
out of the sun upon you like a hawk.

And suddenly you're through, arraigned yet freed,
as if you'd passed from behind a waterfall
on the black current of a tarmac road

past armour-plated vehicles, out between
the posted soldiers flowing and receding
like tree shadows into the polished windscreen.

The Haw Lantern

The wintry haw is burning out of season,
crab of the thorn, a small light for small people,
wanting no more from them but that they keep
the wick of self-respect from dying out,
not having to blind them with illumination.

But sometimes when your breath plumes in the frost
it takes the roaming shape of Diogenes
with his lantern, seeking one just man;
so you end up scrutinized from behind the haw
he holds up at eye-level on its twig,
and you flinch before its bonded pith and stone,
its blood-prick that you wish would test and clear you,
its pecked-at ripeness that scans you, then moves on.

The Stone Grinder

Penelope worked with some guarantee of a plot.
Whatever she unweaved at night
might advance it all by a day.

Me, I ground the same stones for fifty years
and what I undid was never the thing I had done.
I was unrewarded as darkness at a mirror.

I prepared my surface to survive what came over it –
cartographers, printmakers, all that lining and inking.
I ordained opacities and they haruspicated.

For them it was a new start and a clean slate
every time. For me, it was coming full circle
like the ripple perfected in stillness.

So. To commemorate me. Imagine the faces
stripped off the face of a quarry. Practise
coitus interruptus on a pile of old lithographs.

A Daylight Art

for Norman MacCaig

On the day he was to take the poison
Socrates told his friends he had been writing:
putting Aesop's fables into verse.

And this was not because Socrates loved wisdom
and advocated the examined life.
The reason was that he had had a dream.

Caesar, now, or Herod or Constantine
or any number of Shakespearean kings
bursting at the end like dams

where original panoramas lie submerged
which have to rise again before the death scenes –
you can believe in their believing dreams.

But hardly Socrates. Until, that is,
he tells his friends the dream had kept recurring
all his life, repeating one instruction:

Practise the art, which art until that moment
he always took to mean philosophy.
Happy the man, therefore, with a natural gift

for practising the right one from the start –
poetry, say, or fishing; whose nights are dreamless;
whose deep-sunk panoramas rise and pass

like daylight through the rod's eye or the nib's eye.

Parable Island

I

Although they are an occupied nation
and their only border is an inland one
they yield to nobody in their belief
that the country is an island.

Somewhere in the far north, in a region
every native thinks of as 'the coast',
there lies the mountain of the shifting names.

The occupiers call it Cape Basalt.
The Sun's Headstone, say farmers in the east.
Drunken westerners call it The Orphan's Tit.

To find out where he stands the traveller
has to keep listening – since there is no map
which draws the line he knows he must have crossed.

Meanwhile, the forked-tongued natives keep repeating
prophecies they pretend not to believe
about a point where all the names converge
underneath the mountain and where (some day)
they are going to start to mine the ore of truth.

II

In the beginning there was one bell-tower
which struck its single note each day at noon
in honour of the one-eyed all-creator.

At least, this was the original idea
missionary scribes record they found
in autochthonous tradition. But even there

you can't be sure that parable is not
at work already retrospectively,
since all their early manuscripts are full

of stylized eye-shapes and recurrent glosses
in which those old revisionists derive
the word *island* from roots in *eye* and *land*.

III
Now archaeologists begin to gloss the glosses.
To one school, the stone circles are pure symbol;
to another, assembly spots or hut foundations.

One school thinks a post-hole in an ancient floor
stands first of all for a pupil in an iris.
The other thinks a post-hole is a post-hole. And so on –

like the subversives and collaborators
always vying with a fierce possessiveness
for the right to set 'the island story' straight.

IV
The elders dream of boat-journeys and havens
and have their stories too, like the one about the man
who took to his bed, it seems, and died convinced

that the cutting of the Panama Canal
would mean the ocean would all drain away
and the island disappear by aggrandizement.

11

From the Republic of Conscience

I

When I landed in the republic of conscience
it was so noiseless when the engines stopped
I could hear a curlew high above the runway.

At immigration, the clerk was an old man
who produced a wallet from his homespun coat
and showed me a photograph of my grandfather.

The woman in customs asked me to declare
the words of our traditional cures and charms
to heal dumbness and avert the evil eye.

No porters. No interpreter. No taxi.
You carried your own burden and very soon
your symptoms of creeping privilege disappeared.

II

Fog is a dreaded omen there but lightning
spells universal good and parents hang
swaddled infants in trees during thunderstorms.

Salt is their precious mineral. And seashells
are held to the ear during births and funerals.
The base of all inks and pigments is seawater.

Their sacred symbol is a stylized boat.
The sail is an ear, the mast a sloping pen,
The hull a mouth-shape, the keel an open eye.

At their inauguration, public leaders
must swear to uphold unwritten law and weep
to atone for their presumption to hold office –

and to affirm their faith that all life sprang
from salt in tears which the sky-god wept
after he dreamt his solitude was endless.

III

I came back from that frugal republic
with my two arms the one length, the customs woman
having insisted my allowance was myself.

The old man rose and gazed into my face
and said that was official recognition
that I was now a dual citizen.

He therefore desired me when I got home
to consider myself a representative
and to speak on their behalf in my own tongue.

Their embassies, he said, were everywhere
but operated independently
and no ambassador would ever be relieved.

Hailstones

I

My cheek was hit and hit:
sudden hailstones
pelted and bounced on the road.

When it cleared again
something whipped and knowledgeable
had withdrawn

and left me there with my chances.
I made a small hard ball
of burning water running from my hand

just as I make this now
out of the melt of the real thing
smarting into its absence.

II

To be reckoned with, all the same,
those brats of showers.
The way they refused permission,

rattling the classroom window
like a ruler across the knuckles,
the way they were perfect first

and then in no time dirty slush.
Thomas Traherne had his orient wheat
for proof and wonder

but for us, it was the sting of hailstones
and the unstingable hands of Eddie Diamond
foraging in the nettles.

III

Nipple and hive, bite-lumps,
small acorns of the almost pleasurable
intimated and disallowed

when the shower ended
and everything said *wait*.
For what? For forty years

to say there, there you had
the truest foretaste of your aftermath –
in that dilation

when the light opened in silence
and a car with wipers going still
laid perfect tracks in the slush.

Two Quick Notes

I

My old hard friend, how you sought
Occasions of justified anger!
Who could buff me like you

Who wanted the soul to ring true
And plain as a galvanized bucket
And would kick it to test it?

Or whack it clean like a carpet.
So of course when you turned on yourself
You were ferocious.

II

Abrupt and thornproofed and lonely.
A raider from the old country
Of night prayer and principled challenge,

Crashing at barriers
You thought ought still to be there,
Overshooting into thin air.

O upright self-wounding prie-dieu
In shattered free fall:
Hail and farewell.

The Stone Verdict

When he stands in the judgment place
With his stick in his hand and the broad hat
Still on his head, maimed by self-doubt
And an old disdain of sweet talk and excuses,
It will be no justice if the sentence is blabbed out.
He will expect more than words in the ultimate court
He relied on through a lifetime's speechlessness.

Let it be like the judgment of Hermes,
God of the stone heap, where the stones were verdicts
Cast solidly at his feet, piling up around him
Until he stood waist deep in the cairn
Of his apotheosis: maybe a gate-pillar
Or a tumbled wallstead where hogweed earths the silence
Somebody will break at last to say, 'Here
His spirit lingers,' and will have said too much.

From the Land of the Unspoken

I have heard of a bar of platinum
kept by a logical and talkative nation
as their standard of measurement,
the throne room and the burial chamber
of every calculation and prediction.
I could feel at home inside that metal core
slumbering at the very hub of systems.

We are a dispersed people whose history
is a sensation of opaque fidelity.
When or why our exile began
among the speech-ridden, we cannot tell
but solidarity comes flooding up in us
when we hear their legends of infants discovered
floating in coracles towards destiny
or of kings' biers heaved and borne away
on the river's shoulders or out into the sea roads.

When we recognize our own, we fall in step
but do not altogether come up level.
My deepest contact was underground
strap-hanging back to back on a rush-hour train
and in a museum once, I inhaled
vernal assent from a neck and shoulder
pretending to be absorbed in a display
of absolutely silent quernstones.

Our unspoken assumptions have the force
of revelation. How else could we know
that whoever is the first of us to seek
assent and votes in a rich democracy
will be the last of us and have killed our language?
Meanwhile, if we miss the sight of a fish
we heard jumping and then see its ripples,
that means one more of us is dying somewhere.

A Ship of Death

Scyld was still a strong man when his time came
and he crossed over into Our Lord's keeping.
His warrior band did what he bade them
when he laid down the law among the Danes:
they shouldered him out to the sea's flood,
the chief they revered who had long ruled them.
A ring-necked prow rode in the harbour,
clad with ice, its cables tightening.
They stretched their beloved lord in the boat,
laid out amidships by the mast
the great ring-giver. Far-fetched treasures
were piled upon him, and precious gear.
I never heard before of a ship so well furbished
with battle-tackle, bladed weapons
and coats of mail. The treasure was massed
on top of him: it would travel far
on out into the sway of ocean.
They decked his body no less bountifully
with offerings than those first ones did
who cast him away when he was a child
and launched him out alone over the waves.
And they set a gold standard up
high above his head and let him drift
to wind and tide, bewailing him
and mourning their loss. No man can tell,
no wise man in the hall or weathered veteran
knows for certain who salvaged that load.

Beowulf, ll., 26–52

The Spoonbait

So a new similitude is given us
And we say: The soul may be compared

Unto a spoonbait that a child discovers
Beneath the sliding lid of a pencil case,

Glimpsed once and imagined for a lifetime
Risen and free and spooling out of nowhere –

A shooting star going back up the darkness.
It flees him and it burns him all at once

Like the single drop that Dives implored
Falling and falling into a great gulf.

Then exit, the polished helmet of a hero
Laid out amidships above scudding water.

Exit, alternatively, a toy of light
Reeled through him upstream, snagging on nothing.

In Memoriam: Robert Fitzgerald

The socket of each axehead like the squared
Doorway to a megalithic tomb
With its slabbed passage that keeps opening forward
To face another corbelled stone-faced door
That opens on a third. There is no last door,
Just threshold stone, stone jambs, stone crossbeam
Repeating *enter, enter, enter, enter.*
Lintel and upright fly past in the dark.

After the bowstring sang a swallow's note,
The arrow whose migration is its mark
Leaves a whispered breath in every socket.
The great test over, while the gut's still humming,
This time it travels out of all knowing
Perfectly aimed towards the vacant centre.

The Old Team

Dusk. Scope of air. A railed pavilion
Formal and blurring in the sepia
Of (always) summery Edwardian
Ulster. Which could be India
Or England. Or any old parade ground
Where a moustachioed tenantry togged out
To pose with folded arms, all musclebound
And staunch and forever up against it.

Moyola Park FC! Sons of Castledawson!
Stokers and scutchers! Grandfather McCann!
Team spirit, walled parkland, the linen mill
Have, in your absence, grown historical
As those lightly clapped, dull-thumping games of football.
The steady coffins sail past at eye-level.

Clearances

in memoriam M.K.H., 1911–1984

She taught me what her uncle once taught her:
How easily the biggest coal block split
If you got the grain and hammer angled right.

The sound of that relaxed alluring blow,
Its co-opted and obliterated echo,
Taught me to hit, taught me to loosen,

Taught me between the hammer and the block
To face the music. Teach me now to listen,
To strike it rich behind the linear black.

1

A cobble thrown a hundred years ago
Keeps coming at me, the first stone
Aimed at a great-grandmother's turncoat brow.
The pony jerks and the riot's on.
She's crouched low in the trap
Running the gauntlet that first Sunday
Down the brae to Mass at a panicked gallop.
He whips on through the town to cries of 'Lundy!'

Call her 'The Convert'. 'The Exogamous Bride'.
Anyhow, it is a genre piece
Inherited on my mother's side
And mine to dispose with now she's gone.
Instead of silver and Victorian lace,
The exonerating, exonerated stone.

2

Polished linoleum shone there. Brass taps shone.
The china cups were very white and big –
An unchipped set with sugar bowl and jug.
The kettle whistled. Sandwich and teascone
Were present and correct. In case it run,
The butter must be kept out of the sun.
And don't be dropping crumbs. Don't tilt your chair.
Don't reach. Don't point. Don't make noise when you stir.

It is Number 5, New Row, Land of the Dead,
Where grandfather is rising from his place
With spectacles pushed back on a clean bald head
To welcome a bewildered homing daughter
Before she even knocks. 'What's this? What's this?'
And they sit down in the shining room together.

3

When all the others were away at Mass
I was all hers as we peeled potatoes.
They broke the silence, let fall one by one
Like solder weeping off the soldering iron:
Cold comforts set between us, things to share
Gleaming in a bucket of clean water.
And again let fall. Little pleasant splashes
From each other's work would bring us to our senses.

So while the parish priest at her bedside
Went hammer and tongs at the prayers for the dying
And some were responding and some crying
I remembered her head bent towards my head,
Her breath in mine, our fluent dipping knives –
Never closer the whole rest of our lives.

4

Fear of affectation made her affect
Inadequacy whenever it came to
Pronouncing words 'beyond her'. *Bertold Brek.*
She'd manage something hampered and askew
Every time, as if she might betray
The hampered and inadequate by too
Well-adjusted a vocabulary.
With more challenge than pride, she'd tell me, 'You
Know all them things.' So I governed my tongue
In front of her, a genuinely well-
adjusted adequate betrayal
Of what I knew better. I'd *naw* and *aye*
And decently relapse into the wrong
Grammar which kept us allied and at bay.

5

The cool that came off sheets just off the line
Made me think the damp must still be in them
But when I took my corners of the linen
And pulled against her, first straight down the hem
And then diagonally, then flapped and shook
The fabric like a sail in a cross-wind,
They made a dried-out undulating thwack.
So we'd stretch and fold and end up hand to hand
For a split second as if nothing had happened
For nothing had that had not always happened
Beforehand, day by day, just touch and go,
Coming close again by holding back
In moves where I was x and she was o
Inscribed in sheets she'd sewn from ripped-out flour sacks.

6

In the first flush of the Easter holidays
The ceremonies during Holy Week
Were highpoints of our *Sons and Lovers* phase.
The midnight fire. The paschal candlestick.
Elbow to elbow, glad to be kneeling next
To each other up there near the front
Of the packed church, we would follow the text
And rubrics for the blessing of the font.
As the hind longs for the streams, so my soul . . .
Dippings. Towellings. The water breathed on.
The water mixed with chrism and with oil.
Cruet tinkle. Formal incensation
And the psalmist's outcry taken up with pride:
Day and night my tears have been my bread.

7

In the last minutes he said more to her
Almost than in all their life together.
'You'll be in New Row on Monday night
And I'll come up for you and you'll be glad
When I walk in the door . . . Isn't that right?'
His head was bent down to her propped-up head.
She could not hear but we were overjoyed.
He called her good and girl. Then she was dead,
The searching for a pulsebeat was abandoned
And we all knew one thing by being there.
The space we stood around had been emptied
Into us to keep, it penetrated
Clearances that suddenly stood open.
High cries were felled and a pure change happened.

8

I thought of walking round and round a space
Utterly empty, utterly a source
Where the decked chestnut tree had lost its place
In our front hedge above the wallflowers.
The white chips jumped and jumped and skited high.
I heard the hatchet's differentiated
Accurate cut, the crack, the sigh
And collapse of what luxuriated
Through the shocked tips and wreckage of it all.
Deep planted and long gone, my coeval
Chestnut from a jam jar in a hole,
Its heft and hush become a bright nowhere,
A soul ramifying and forever
Silent, beyond silence listened for.

The Milk Factory

Scuts of froth swirled from the discharge pipe.
We halted on the other bank and watched
A milky water run from the pierced side
Of milk itself, the crock of its substance spilt
Across white limbo floors where shift-workers
Waded round the clock, and the factory
Kept its distance like a bright-decked star-ship.

There we go, soft-eyed calves of the dew,
Astonished and assumed into fluorescence.

The Summer of Lost Rachel

Potato crops are flowering,
    Hard green plums appear
On damson trees at your back door
    And every berried briar

Is glittering and dripping
    Whenever showers plout down
On flooded hay and flooding drills.
    There's a ring around the moon.

The whole summer was waterlogged
    Yet everyone is loath
To trust the rain's soft-soaping ways
    And sentiments of growth

Because all confidence in summer's
    Unstinting largesse
Broke down last May when we laid you out
    In white, your whited face

Gashed from the accident, but still,
    So absolutely still,
And the setting sun set merciless
    And every merciful

Register inside us yearned
    To run the film back,
For you to step into the road
    Wheeling your bright-rimmed bike,

34

Safe and sound as usual,
    Across, then down the lane,
The twisted spokes all straightened out,
    The awful skid-marks gone.

But no. So let the downpours flood
    Our memory's riverbed
Until, in thick-webbed currents,
    The life you might have led

Wavers and tugs dreamily
    As soft-plumed waterweed
Which tempts our gaze and quietens it
    And recollects our need.

The Wishing Tree

I thought of her as the wishing tree that died
And saw it lifted, root and branch, to heaven,
Trailing a shower of all that had been driven

Need by need by need into its hale
Sap-wood and bark: coin and pin and nail
Came streaming from it like a comet-tail

New-minted and dissolved. I had a vision
Of an airy branch-head rising through damp cloud,
Of turned-up faces where the tree had stood.

A Postcard from Iceland

As I dipped to test the stream some yards away
From a hot spring, I could hear nothing
But the whole mud-slick muttering and boiling.

And then my guide behind me saying,
'Lukewarm. And I think you'd want to know
That *luk* was an old Icelandic word for hand.'

And you would want to know (but you know already)
How usual that waft and pressure felt
When the inner palm of water found my palm.

A Peacock's Feather

for Daisy Garnett

Six days ago the water fell
To christen you, to work its spell
And wipe your slate, we hope, for good.
But now your life is sleep and food
Which, with the touch of love, suffice
You, Daisy, Daisy, English niece.

Gloucestershire: its prospects lie
Wooded and misty to my eye
Whose landscape, as your mother's was,
Is other than this mellowness
Of topiary, lawn and brick,
Possessed, untrespassed, walled, nostalgic.

I come from scraggy farm and moss,
Old patchworks that the pitch and toss
Of history have left dishevelled.
But here, for your sake, I have levelled
My cart-track voice to garden tones,
Cobbled the bog with Cotswold stones.

Ravelling strands of families mesh
In love-knots of two minds, one flesh.
The future's not our own. We'll weave
An in-law maze, we'll nod and wave
With trust but little intimacy –
So this is a billet-doux to say

That in a warm July you lay
Christened and smiling in Bradley
While I, a guest in your green court,
At a west window sat and wrote
Self-consciously in gathering dark.
I might as well be in Coole Park.

So before I leave your ordered home,
Let us pray. May tilth and loam,
Darkened with Celts' and Saxons' blood,
Breastfeed your love of house and wood –
Where I drop this for you, as I pass,
Like the peacock's feather on the grass.

1972

Grotus and Coventina

Far from home Grotus dedicated an altar to Coventina
Who holds in her right hand a waterweed
And in her left a pitcher spilling out a river.
Anywhere Grotus looked at running water he felt at home
And when he remembered the stone where he cut his name
Some dried-up course beneath his breastbone started
Pouring and darkening – more or less the way
The thought of his stunted altar works on me.

Remember when our electric pump gave out,
Priming it with bucketfuls, our idiotic rage
And hangdog phone-calls to the farm next door
For somebody please to come and fix it?
And when it began to hammer on again,
Jubilation at the tap's full force, the sheer
Given fact of water, how you felt you'd never
Waste one drop but know its worth better always.
Do you think we could run through all that one more time?
I'll be Grotus, you be Coventina.

Holding Course

Propellers underwater, cabins drumming, lights –
Unthought-of but constant out there every night,
The big ferries pondered on their courses.
I envy you your sight of them this morning,
Docked and massive with their sloped-back funnels.

The outlook is high and airy where you stand
By our attic window. Far Toledo blues.
And from a shelf behind you
The alpine thistle we brought from Covadonga
Inclines its jaggy crest.

Last autumn we were smouldering and parched
As those spikes that keep vigil overhead
Like Grendel's steely talon nailed
To the mead-hall roof. And then we broke through
Or we came through. It was its own reward.

We are voluptuaries of the morning after.
As gulls cry out above the deep channels
And you stand on and on, twiddling your hair,
Think of me as your MacWhirr of the boudoir,
Head on, one track, ignorant of manoeuvre.

The Song of the Bullets

I watched a long time in the yard
    The usual stars, the still
And seemly planets, lantern-bright
    Above our darkened hill.

And then a star that moved, I thought,
    For something moved indeed
Up from behind the massed skyline
    At ardent silent speed

And when it reached the zenith, cut
    Across the curving path
Of a second light that swung up like
    A scythe-point through its swathe.

'The sky at night is full of us',
    Now one began to sing,
'Our slugs of lead lie cold and dead,
    Our trace is on the wing.

Our casings and our blunted parts
    Are gathered up below
As justice stands aghast and stares
    Like the sun on arctic snow.

Our guilt was accidental. Blame,
    Blame because you must.
Then blame young men for semen or
    Blame the moon for moondust.'

As ricochets that warble close,
  Then die away on wind,
That hard contralto sailed across
  And stellar quiet reigned

Until the other fireball spoke:
  'We are the iron will.
We hoop and cooper worlds beyond
  The killer and the kill.

Mount Olivet's beatitudes,
  The soul's cadenced desires
Cannot prevail against us who
  Dwell in the marbled fires

Of every steady eye that ever
  Narrowed, sighted, paused:
We fire and glaze the shape of things
  Until the shape's imposed.'

Now wind was blowing through the yard.
  Clouds blanked the stars. The still
And seemly planets disappeared
  Above our darkened hill.

Wolfe Tone

Light as a skiff, manoeuvrable
yet outmanoeuvred,

I affected epaulettes and a cockade,
wrote a style well-bred and impervious

to the solidarity I angled for,
and played the ancient Roman with a razor.

I was the shouldered oar that ended up
far from the brine and whiff of venture,

like a scratching-post or a crossroads flagpole,
out of my element among small farmers –

I who once wakened to the shouts of men
rising from the bottom of the sea,

men in their shirts mounting through deep water
when the Atlantic stove our cabin's dead lights in

and the big fleet split and Ireland dwindled
as we ran before the gale under bare poles.

A Shooting Script

They are riding away from whatever might have been
Towards what will never be, in a held shot:
Teachers on bicycles, saluting native speakers,
Treading the nineteen-twenties like the future.

Still pedalling out at the end of the lens,
Not getting anywhere and not getting away.
Mix to fuchsia that 'follows the language'.
A long soundless sequence. Pan and fade.

Then voices over, in different Irishes,
Discussing translation jobs and rates per line;
Like nineteenth-century milestones in grass verges,
Occurrence of names like R. M. Ballantyne.

A close-up on the cat's eye of a button
Pulling back wide to the cape of a soutane,
Biretta, Roman collar, Adam's apple.
Freeze his blank face. Let the credits run

And just when it looks as if it is all over –
Tracking shots of a long wave up a strand
That breaks towards the point of a stick writing and writing
Words in the old script in the running sand.

From the Canton of Expectation

I

We lived deep in a land of optative moods,
under high, banked clouds of resignation.
A rustle of loss in the phrase *Not in our lifetime*,
the broken nerve when we prayed *Vouchsafe* or *Deign*,
were creditable, sufficient to the day.

Once a year we gathered in a field
of dance platforms and tents where children sang
songs they had learned by rote in the old language.
An auctioneer who had fought in the brotherhood
enumerated the humiliations
we always took for granted, but not even he
considered this, I think, a call to action.
Iron-mouthed loudspeakers shook the air
yet nobody felt blamed. He had confirmed us.
When our rebel anthem played the meeting shut
we turned for home and the usual harassment
by militiamen on overtime at roadblocks.

II

And next thing, suddenly, this change of mood.
Books open in the newly-wired kitchens.
Young heads that might have dozed a life away
against the flanks of milking cows were busy
paving and pencilling their first causeways
across the prescribed texts. The paving stones
of quadrangles came next and a grammar
of imperatives, the new age of demands.

They would banish the conditional for ever,
this generation born impervious to
the triumph in our cries of *de profundis*.
Our faith in winning by enduring most
they made anathema, intelligences
brightened and unmannerly as crowbars.

III

What looks the strongest has outlived its term.
The future lies with what's affirmed from under.
These things that corroborated us when we dwelt
under the aegis of our stealthy patron,
the guardian angel of passivity,
now sink a fang of menace in my shoulder.
I repeat the word 'stricken' to myself
and stand bareheaded under the banked clouds
edged more and more with brassy thunderlight.
I yearn for hammerblows on clinkered planks,
the uncompromised report of driven thole-pins,
to know there is one among us who never swerved
from all his instincts told him was right action,
who stood his ground in the indicative,
whose boat will lift when the cloudburst happens.

The Mud Vision

Statues with exposed hearts and barbed-wire crowns
Still stood in alcoves, hares flitted beneath
The dozing bellies of jets, our menu-writers
And punks with aerosol sprays held their own
With the best of them. Satellite link-ups
Wafted over us the blessings of popes, heliports
Maintained a charmed circle for idols on tour
And casualties on their stretchers. We sleepwalked
The line between panic and formulae, screentested
Our first native models and the last of the mummers,
Watching ourselves at a distance, advantaged
And airy as a man on a springboard
Who keeps limbering up because the man cannot dive.

And then in the foggy midlands it appeared,
Our mud vision, as if a rose window of mud
Had invented itself out of the glittery damp,
A gossamer wheel, concentric with its own hub
Of nebulous dirt, sullied yet lucent.
We had heard of the sun standing still and the sun
That changed colour, but we were vouchsafed
Original clay, transfigured and spinning.
And then the sunsets ran murky, the wiper
Could never entirely clean off the windscreen,
Reservoirs tasted of silt, a light fuzz
Accrued in the hair and the eyebrows, and some
Took to wearing a smudge on their foreheads
To be prepared for whatever. Vigils
Began to be kept around puddled gaps,
On altars bulrushes ousted the lilies

And a rota of invalids came and went
On beds they could lease placed in range of the shower.

A generation who had seen a sign!
Those nights when we stood in an·umber dew and smelled
Mould in the verbena, or woke to a light
Furrow-breath on the pillow, when the talk
Was all about who had seen it and our fear
Was touched with a secret pride, only ourselves
Could be adequate then to our lives. When the rainbow
Curved flood-brown and ran like a water-rat's back
So that drivers on the hard shoulder switched off to watch,
We wished it away, and yet we presumed it a test
That would prove us beyond expectation.

We lived, of course, to learn the folly of that.
One day it was gone and the east gable
Where its trembling corolla had balanced
Was starkly a ruin again, with dandelions
Blowing high up on the ledges, and moss
That slumbered on through its increase. As cameras raked
The site from every angle, experts
Began their *post factum* jabber and all of us
Crowded in tight for the big explanations.
Just like that, we forgot that the vision was ours,
Our one chance to know the incomparable
And dive to a future. What might have been origin
We dissipated in news. The clarified place
Had retrieved neither us nor itself – except
You could say we survived. So say that, and watch us
Who had our chance to be mud-men, convinced and estranged,
Figure in our own eyes for the eyes of the world.

The Disappearing Island

Once we presumed to found ourselves for good
Between its blue hills and those sandless shores
Where we spent our desperate night in prayer and vigil,

Once we had gathered driftwood, made a hearth
And hung our cauldron like a firmament,
The island broke beneath us like a wave.

The land sustaining us seemed to hold firm
Only when we embraced it *in extremis*.
All I believe that happened there was vision.

The Riddle

You never saw it used but still can hear
The sift and fall of stuff hopped on the mesh,

Clods and buds in a little dust-up,
The dribbled pile accruing under it.

Which would be better, what sticks or what falls through?
Or does the choice itself create the value?

Legs apart, deft-handed, start a mime
To sift the sense of things from what's imagined

And work out what was happening in that story
Of the man who carried water in a riddle.

Was it culpable ignorance, or was it rather
A *via negativa* through drops and let-downs?

Notes

PAGE 4

hoke: To root, to grub; *march:* boundary

PAGE 21

spoonbait: An angler's lure shaped like the bowl of a spoon

PAGE 23

Moyola Park FC: The local football club at Castledawson

PAGE 25

Lundy: Governor of Derry in 1689. The name is used contemptuously by Ulster Orangemen to signify a traitor to their cause

PAGE 40

Coventina: A water divinity whose cult was observed by soldiers along Hadrian's Wall

PAGE 41

MacWhirr: The main character in Joseph Conrad's *Typhoon*